DISCOVERING THE NEW WORLD

EXPLORERS AND AMERICAN INDIANS

by John Micklos, Jr.

Consultant:
Richard Bell
Associate Professor of History
University of Maryland, College Park

CAPSTONE PRESS
a capstone imprint

Connect Books are published by Capstone Press,
1710 Roe Crest Drive, North Mankato, Minnesota 56003
www.mycapstone.com

Library of Congress Cataloging-in-Publication Data

Names: Micklos, John, author.
Title: Explorers and American Indians / by John Micklos, Jr.
Description: North Mankato, Minnesota : Capstone Press, 2017. | Series:
  Connect. Discovering the new world | Includes bibliographical references
  and index. | Audience: Ages 9–11. | Audience: Grade 4 to 6.
Identifiers: LCCN 2015044190|
  ISBN 9781515718666 (library binding) |
  ISBN 9781515718697 (paperback) |
  ISBN 9781515718727 (eBook PDF)
Subjects: LCSH: North America—Discovery and exploration—Juvenile
  literature. | Indians—First contact with Europeans—Juvenile literature.
  | Indians of North America—History—Juvenile literature.
Classification: LCC E45 .M53 2017 | DDC 970.004/97—dc23
LC record available at http://lccn.loc.gov/2015044190

Editorial Credits

Brenda Haugen and Alesha Halvorson, editors; Ted Williams, designer;
Kelly Garvin, media researcher; Laura Manthe, production specialist

Photo Credits

Alamy/Glasshouse Images, 38-39; Corbis/GraphicalArtis, cover; Getty Images: David
David Gallery, 27, Print Collector, 15, Stock Montage, 18, Superstock, 23; Newscom:
akg-images, 4-5, 7, Album/Prisma, 32, Piero Oliosi/Polaris, 11, World History Archive,
36-37; North Wind Picture Archive, 9, 12, 17, 21, 24, 29, 30-31, 35, 40-41, 43; The
Image Works/J.Bedmar/Iberfoto, 45

Artistic Elements: Shutterstock: Adam Gryko, Caesart, ilolab, Joanna Dorota,
Picsfive

Printed and bound in Canada.
009648F16

-CHAPTER ONE-

Surprises

Imagine the surprise when Europeans and American Indians first met on the shores of the Americas more than 500 years ago. From the late 1400s into the early 1600s, many explorers crossed the Atlantic Ocean from Europe. As explorers arrived, many American Indian tribes experienced the shock of seeing strange men enter their harbors. The strangers traveled on huge brown wooden boats with large sails. Some tribes described the boats as floating islands. The strangers had pale white skin. They dressed in strange, fancy clothing. Strangest of all, they had hair over much of their faces and bodies.

Explorers called the land they reached the New World.

But not all of the American Indian tribes were surprised at seeing these white strangers. Some tribes, such as the Algonquin (*al-GONG-kin*), had heard **prophecies** that white men would one day come from the east. Many tribes first welcomed the strange-looking people in their massive boats with a mixture of friendship and awe. A few feared the newcomers and greeted the white men with arrows.

The explorers who first reached the coastlines of what are now North America and Central America faced their own surprises. Some sought a route to the Far East. Others sought gold and silver. Although they did not find precious metals, they did discover new crops and other trade goods that would have great value in Europe.

prophecy—a prediction of something to come

Explorers crossed the Atlantic Ocean from countries such as England, France, and Spain.

Relations between explorers and American Indians often began peacefully with trade. The Europeans traded items such as glass beads and metal objects. Some explorers tried to establish settlements. The American Indians usually didn't mind—as long as the white men did not disturb their hunting or fishing grounds. Other explorers came to conquer the people they met. They burned villages, captured slaves, and took whatever items they could use.

Many European explorers viewed the native people as **inferior**. Most North and Central American tribes had well-organized societies. But American Indian life was very different from European life. Some tribes dressed in animal skins or loincloths. Some moved from place to place as they hunted and fished. European explorers did not try to understand or appreciate this way of life.

Samuel de Champlain, an early French explorer, called the American Indians he met "sauvages." In French this meant "wild" or "savage." Most Europeans viewed the "savages" of North America as uncivilized and fierce. When native peoples fought against white settlers invading their lands, their attacks were often described as being savage. But the American Indians certainly had cause for anger.

Depending on the location, the American Indians traded goods such as furs or cotton.

How do we know about these first **encounters** between European explorers and native tribes? Some explorers kept detailed records of their travels. Most American Indian tribes, on the other hand, had no written language. Their stories were passed down by word of mouth across generations. They were not written down until centuries later, if at all. Sometimes the American Indian side has been told through the accounts of the explorers. But then the comments are filtered through the explorers' eyes. More recent writings offer a more balanced view. Still, there is little that reflects first-hand American Indian perspectives. But one thing is for sure. These first encounters were life-changing experiences for everyone involved.

inferior—lower in rank or status

encounter—an unexpected or difficult meeting

-CHAPTER TWO-

Disappointment and Fascination

Disappointment. That's probably what Christopher Columbus felt when he arrived in the New World from Spain on October 12, 1492. He had hoped to reach Asia. He expected to find people dressed in fine clothes. Instead he was greeted by naked members of the Taino (*TYE-no*) tribe in an area now known as the Bahamas.

The land Columbus thought he "discovered" had been home to the Taino for many years. They had a well-developed culture with towns spread across many islands. Talented artists, the Taino made pottery, wove belts from dyed cotton, and carved images into wood and stone. They also "built oceangoing canoes large enough for more than 100 paddlers."

In his ship's record book, Columbus commented on the "handsome bodies and very fine faces" of the Taino. He noted the ways they painted their faces and bodies. The Taino had never seen iron products. "I showed them swords and they grasped them by the blade and cut themselves through ignorance," Columbus wrote. A peaceful people, the Taino used clubs and bows and arrows as weapons for defense against enemies.

Despite not finding what he wanted, Columbus claimed possession of the island for the king and queen of Spain. The Taino likely didn't realize Columbus claimed the land. Soon lively trading began. The Taino traded parrots and cotton thread. The Spaniards traded tiny metal bells and glass beads.

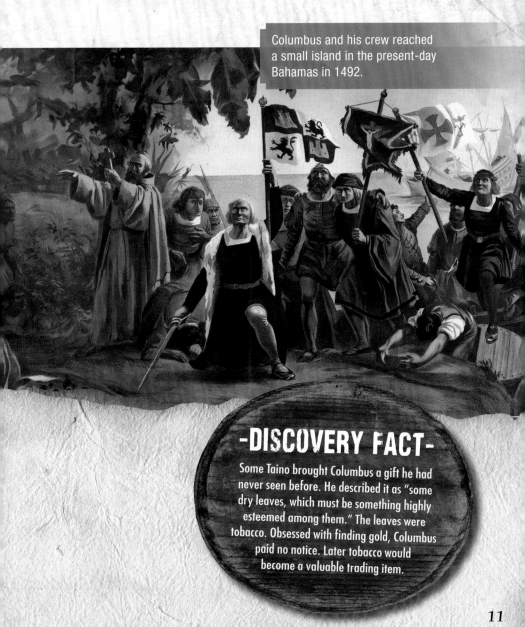

Columbus and his crew reached a small island in the present-day Bahamas in 1492.

-DISCOVERY FACT-

Some Taino brought Columbus a gift he had never seen before. He described it as "some dry leaves, which must be something highly esteemed among them." The leaves were tobacco. Obsessed with finding gold, Columbus paid no notice. Later tobacco would become a valuable trading item.

The Taino people seemed fascinated by the bearded white strangers and their big wooden ships. By the second day, hundreds of Taino crowded the beach. Many rowed to Columbus's ships in large canoes. Now it was the Europeans' turn to be surprised. They had never seen anything quite like the wooden paddles the Taino used to propel their canoes. Over the years, the explorers learned many new things from American Indians. But many explorers failed to appreciate the skills and knowledge of the native people.

Columbus noted that the people he met shared everything they received. One evening Columbus invited a Taino chief for dinner onboard ship. The chief tasted only a small sample of each dish. Then he "sent the rest to his people," Columbus wrote.

Soon Columbus strained relations by capturing several of the men who visited his ship. He wanted them to direct him to the next set of islands. He also wanted to take some of them back to Spain. He planned to present them to King Ferdinand and Queen Isabella. He was upset when the men escaped. But when a man came to trade with the Spanish on their next stop, Columbus gave him presents. Columbus wanted the man to "give a good account of us."

The Taino people traded goods with Columbus and his crew.

When they reached what is now Cuba, the Spaniards found larger villages. The advance party received a royal welcome. They reported that the Taino people here "kissed their hands and feet, marveling and believing that they came from the sky."

Next Columbus sailed south and east to the island of Hispaniola. There Taino villagers carried Columbus and his men across rivers and through muddy places. At a large village, the tribal leader led Columbus to a chair on a raised platform. Then he took off his crown and placed it on Columbus's head. In return Columbus gave the leader shoes and a silver ring.

Columbus returned to Spain from his first **expedition** to the New World after just five months. He had failed to find riches. He never really understood what he *had* found. He believed he had reached islands near Asia. As historian William Least Heat Moon says, Columbus believed "he had gone where he had not gone and done what he had not done." What Columbus did accomplish was to start an exchange "of foods, technologies, arts, ways of thought." The wave of European contact that Columbus began would forever change the North American continent and the lives of the people who lived there.

expedition—a journey with a goal, such as exploring or searching for something

Columbus was crowned by a Taino chief during his expedition in Hispaniola.

-CHAPTER THREE-

Canadian Encounters

Jacques Cartier first came to the New World from France in 1534. He began exploring around the mouth of the St. Lawrence River in what is now the province of Quebec, Canada. Cartier tried to make friends with the Huron (*HYOO-ruhn*) people he met. He wanted to trade for the furs of the animals they trapped. Cartier also admired the bravery and strength of the Huron. In his diary Cartier described how one Huron carried him from his boat to shore as if he were a child.

The Huron grew less friendly after Cartier raised a large cross. Chief Donnacona angrily pointed to the cross and then to the ground. He made it clear that "Cartier and the French were trespassers."

The Huron were awed by European technology. Chief Donnacona asked to see how Cartier's cannons worked. The Huron were amazed at these weapons whose metal balls could crush trees—and men. But the Huron would soon amaze the explorers with knowledge of their own.

The Huron people were unhappy when Cartier erected a large cross on the St. Lawrence River in present-day Quebec in 1534.

17

Jacques Cartier

On Cartier's second voyage in 1535, Huron medicine saved him and many of his men from death. Cartier's ships sat icebound for months in the St. Lawrence River near what is now the city of Quebec. Twenty-five men died. Nearly all the rest of the crew lay ill. Then a Huron showed the French how to make a medicine by boiling the bark and leaves of an evergreen. Soon Cartier's crew recovered. Cartier wrote that they "recovered health and strength, thanks be to God." Instead, he should have thanked his Huron hosts for their knowledge and help.

In some cases, Cartier tried to respect Huron customs. But during his first journey he invited Chief Donnacona and two of his sons aboard his ship. Then he announced that he planned to take the two boys to France with him. Cartier wanted them to learn French. Then they could serve as interpreters when he returned to the New World. He promised to bring the boys back. Donnacona understood Cartier's desire to train the boys as interpreters. He did not like the way Cartier simply took them, though.

Cartier returned with the two boys in 1535. During this visit, however, he decided to take more Huron people back to France. He kidnapped several tribal members, including Chief Donnacona. He wanted King Francis of France to meet an American Indian leader. Cartier hoped this would boost the king's interest in the New World.

These actions hurt Cartier later. He returned to Canada in 1541 to help form a permanent settlement. None of the Huron returned with him. Most had died in France. Knowing they could not trust Cartier, the Huron refused to help the settlers. Facing challenging conditions and hostile neighbors, the colony failed. After one harsh winter, Cartier returned to France. After another hard year, the other colonists gave up and returned as well.

Cartier took some Hurons with him to France to try and rally support for the exploration of the New World.

-CHAPTER FOUR-

Forming an Alliance

Nearly 70 years after Cartier's journeys, explorer Samuel de Champlain visited some of the same areas in Canada. Champlain admired the simple lives and hunting skills of the American Indian tribes he met. He also admired how they created snowshoes for walking across the snow.

Champlain built a fort at what is now Quebec in 1608. It became a hub for fur trading. Champlain and the other French traders formed an **alliance** with the Huron and Algonquin tribes. The tribes traded furs with Champlain. In return the French helped them fight against their long-time enemies, the Iroquois. For many years, the tribes had battled over land and control of fur trading.

In 1609 Champlain and some of his allies were paddling across a large lake. A group of Iroquois warriors stood on the other side. When these tribes met, they generally fought. The enemies had a **ritual** for battling, which Champlain described in his journal. First Champlain's allies sent some warriors to see if the Iroquois wanted to fight. The Iroquois replied that "as soon as the sun should rise, they would attack us." Warriors from both tribes sang and danced all night getting ready. In the morning the Iroquois moved forward. Three chiefs with headdresses led the way.

The warriors planned to battle with arrows and tomahawks. But Champlain had a **musket**. He fired at the approaching Iroquois chiefs. Loaded with four balls, the gun killed two chiefs and wounded another. "Seeing their chiefs dead, they lost courage and took to flight," Champlain wrote. He named the lake where the battle took place Lake Champlain.

alliance—a union or joining for a common purpose

ritual—a ceremony or special way of doing something

musket—a gun with a long barrel

When Champlain and his allies encountered Iroquois warriors, a deadly battle broke out.

Samuel de Champlain

Several years later Champlain was injured in another battle with the Iroquois. An arrow hit his knee and left him unable to walk. He lived with the Huron that winter and learned more about their culture. Among explorers, Champlain may have had the best relations with the tribes he befriended. Of course, the Iroquois hated him. Champlain's alliance with the Huron and Algonquin tribes led to decades of battles between the Iroquois and the French in North America.

*Some Things Europeans Got
from American Indians*

Corn
Potatoes
Tobacco
Animal furs

---

*Some Things American Indians
Got from the Europeans*

Horses
Peaches
Guns

CHAPTER FIVE

A Prophecy Fulfilled

White men appeared in the harbor of what is now New York City in September 1609. They came on a large wooden ship. The Algonquin Indians were not surprised when Henry Hudson and his crew arrived. Nearly 400 years earlier, Algonquin **prophets** foretold that visitors would come from the east. They even predicted the year based on a series of what they called "cycles" or "fires." The year 1609 was the central year of the central fire.

-DISCOVERY FACT-

Many places have been named after explorers. Here are a few: Lake Champlain; the Hudson River; and Columbus, Ohio.

The prophets disagreed about how the strangers would behave. One thought they would come in peace. He predicted that a new "rainbow" race would emerge from their friendship. Another thought the visitors could bring war. He predicted there could be a disaster unless fears and misunderstandings could be worked out. Others predicted that both types of visitors would come. In that case the Algonquin would face a series of challenges. Their survival would depend on how they reacted. These prophecies were recorded on a special **wampum belt**.

prophet—a person who tells the future

wampum belt—a belt made from polished shells woven together

Hudson and his crew landed on the shore of present-day New York City in 1609.

When Henry Hudson and the crew of the *Half Moon* arrived, more than 200 Algonquins approached. Soon the two groups began trading. The Algonquins were ready for their visitors. They sang songs and told stories that they had prepared for years. They offered tobacco and other gifts. They called Hudson's ship the *Great Floating Bird*.

Hudson and one of his officers, Robert Juet, kept notes about their first meetings with the Algonquin. The Algonquin passed their story along orally across generations. More than 200 years later, their story was finally written down. In 1849 tribal leaders sent a letter to U.S. President Zachary Taylor. The letter described relations between the Algonquin and white settlers over the years. It also detailed what happened during the first meeting.

"Our ancient men, without any delay made a Song concerning their expectation of your coming," said the letter. "Likewise a Drum was made for the purpose, out of the shell of a Sea Turtle." The letter went on to say that the music and dancing "was performed with great solemnity in honor of your coming."

But there was violence as well. Days before the meeting in what is now New York City, some of Hudson's men had **skirmished** with members of a neighboring tribe. One sailor was killed. Then Hudson's crew captured two members of the Canarsie (*ke-NAR-see*) tribe, but they escaped soon after.

skirmish—a small battle

Hudson's ship sailed the Hudson River heading in and beyond New York City.

Hudson continued to travel up what would later be named the Hudson River. He met with Mohican (*moh-HEE-kuhn*) chiefs on September 17. The Mohicans held feasts in honor of Hudson and his crew. Hudson brought some Mohicans aboard his ship. What did the Mohicans think? Two hundred fifty years later, Mohican chief John W. Quinney reported that meeting the strange, pale visitors "overwhelmed the senses" of his ancestors. Other historians say the Mohicans thought the visitors' pale skin meant they were ill.

As Hudson sailed back down the river, he faced angry tribes who knew about his earlier kidnapping of the Canarsie people. Several skirmishes broke out along the way. In one battle, Hudson's men fired muskets and cannons, killing several American Indians.

Soon after, Hudson departed for England. He had planned to come in peace. But he also brought violence. Hudson certainly left the Algonquin **wary** of future European visitors.

wary—cautious, on guard against danger

Hudson's crew had several skirmishes with the native Algonquin people.

-CHAPTER SIX-

A Trail of Blood

By the time Spaniard Hernando de Soto reached Florida in May 1539 in search of riches, he was already a seasoned explorer. In South America, the Incas had one of the world's most highly developed societies. But Spanish weapons and the introduction of European diseases, such as smallpox, allowed the Spaniards to conquer them. De Soto earned a reputation for hunting and killing native people. He personally tortured the Incas' chief general before executing him.

Hernando de Soto became rich as a slave trader in South America. He gained a share of the gold and silver the Spanish took when they conquered the Inca people in Peru.

De Soto anchored near what is now Tampa, Florida. He hoped to find riches in this new land. As small boats set out from the ship, members of the Timucua (*tee-MOO-kwah*) tribe watched from the shore. They sent word for women and children to abandon their villages. They set signal fires to warn others. Their concerns were well founded. Timucua scouts skirmished with the advance party of Spaniards. The scouts killed two Spanish horses but suffered two deaths.

NO FOUNTAIN OF YOUTH

Legend says that Spaniard Juan Ponce de Leon explored Florida searching for the Fountain of Youth. Drinking from these waters was supposed to keep a person from aging. There is no evidence that de Leon's travels were launched to find the mythical fountain. The legend became attached to de Leon after his death. It is almost certainly false. One thing is true, though. De Leon clashed with the Calusa (*kuh-LOO-suh*) tribe. He died in 1521 from an arrow wound suffered in a battle with them.

During the next week, about 600 Spaniards came ashore. So did hundreds of horses and pigs, as well as dogs trained for battle. When de Soto's army moved onward, they found village after village abandoned. The occupants fled into the woods. The Spaniards ate whatever food was left behind. They ransacked the homes looking for gold and silver. They found little.

When they did meet American Indians, de Soto lived up to his reputation. He destroyed village after village. But the American Indians had a strategy for getting rid of him. They told him that wealthy lands lay to the north or west. This caused the Spaniards to keep moving in search of riches.

DEADLY DISEASES

Before Europeans arrived, millions of American Indians lived in what is now the United States and Central and South America. But the Europeans brought diseases such as smallpox, measles, and influenza to the New World. American Indians had no **immunity** to these diseases. Epidemics quickly spread among many tribes. Some tribes were nearly wiped out. Some researchers believe the pigs that de Soto brought along with his army also carried diseases. These diseases may have been later transmitted to the American Indians.

> **immunity**—the ability of the body to resist a disease

Hernando de Soto had a reputation for destroying American Indian villages during his search for riches and gold.

The biggest clash between de Soto and American Indians came in what is now Alabama. Chief Tascalusa of the Mississippians hoped to drive the Spanish away once and for all. He lured de Soto and some of his men into the fortified city of Mabila. Then Tascalusa's warriors attacked. Several thousand Mississippians lost their lives. Although the Spanish won the battle, they lost many soldiers, horses, and supplies. This left them much less dangerous to the tribes they met later, according to historian Roger Carpenter.

A daylong battle between Tascalusa's warriors and de Soto's army left more than 250 Spanish soldiers dead or wounded.

The American Indians simply could not understand why the Spanish were so cruel. According to a Spanish soldier, one chief called de Soto and his men "professional **vagabonds** who wander from place to place, gaining your livelihood by robbing, sacking, and murdering people who give you no offense."

De Soto and his army covered nearly 4,000 miles (6,437 kilometers) through what are now more than 10 southeastern states. De Soto grew ill and died in May 1542. His mission to find riches failed. He left behind a trail of blood.

vagabond—a person who wanders from place to place

CHAPTER SEVEN

A Search for Gold Turns Sour

The Zuni (*ZOO-nee*) people had lived peacefully in their **pueblos** in what is now the southwestern United States for centuries. Their houses were made of adobe, straw, and wood. The Zuni raised corn, beans, cotton, and squash. They hunted deer and other animals. They were skilled at making and decorating pottery.

Coronado led an expedition into the American Southwest in 1540.

Then one day their lives changed forever. An army of Spanish soldiers arrived from Mexico in search of gold. They were led by Francisco Vasquez de Coronado.

A Zuni prophecy stated that invaders would come and conquer their lands. So the coming of strangers was not a total surprise. Still, the Zuni residents of the village of Hawikuh must have been shocked when Coronado's army approached on July 7, 1540. The **conquistadors** had pale faces and thick beards. They wore heavy metal armor. Many carried metal sticks they called muskets that exploded with fire and smoke. Many also rode horses. The Zuni had never seen such weapons or creatures.

pueblo—the Spanish word for village, usually consisting of stone and adobe buildings

conquistador—a leader in the Spanish conquest of North America and South America during the 1500s

-DISCOVERY FACT-

Coronado was impressed with the houses in the Zuni pueblo at Hawikuh. He described them as "very good houses, three, four, and five storeys high, and they have very ... good rooms with corridors, and some quite good apartments."

Coronado sought a rich kingdom named Cíbola. According to legend, the kingdom had seven cities filled with gold. The Spaniards believed Hawikuh was one of those cities. Instead, they were shocked and disappointed by what they found. The only things that matched the legend were "the name of the city and the large stone houses," Coronado reported.

Still, Coronado at first tried to make friends with the Zuni people. He hoped they might know where gold was. According to historian Michael Oberg, the Spaniards worked with American Indians "as long as they had something to fear or to gain from that community."

Up to 700 people lived in a Zuni pueblo.

But when Coronado declared the Zuni subjects of Spain and gave them orders, they resisted. Coronado's troops stormed the pueblo. The Zuni rained arrows down on the Spaniards. But most of the arrows simply bounced off the soldiers' armor.

CHRISTIAN CONVERTS

Some European explorers tried to convert the American Indians they met to Christianity. The various tribes had different spiritual beliefs. Most revolved around a deep respect for nature. White Feather, a Navajo medicine man, summed it up this way: "Not only do we love, honor, and respect our Creator and our Mother Earth, but also every living thing." Few American Indians saw a reason to change and adopt European beliefs. Some explorers used this as a reason to attack them.

Once inside the pueblo, the Spaniards used ladders to reach the Zuni in the higher levels. When Coronado began climbing a ladder, the Zunis hurled rocks down at him. Some of the stones knocked him unconscious for a time. In the end the Spanish prevailed with their guns and horses. The Zunis fled. The Spanish had been low on supplies. They stayed in the town, feasting on the food the Zunis had left behind.

After resting, Coronado's army resumed its search for gold. Next, the troops came to a Hopi (*HOH-pee*) city. The Hopi people knew what had happened to the Zuni tribe. They feared meeting a similar fate. They welcomed the Spaniards and traded with them, but they were eager for the Spaniards to move on.

Once again the Spaniards found no riches. The Hopi steered them farther north and east, saying they would find riches there. This was a way to get Coronado's army to leave their territory and bother other tribes.

In the winter of 1539–1540, Coronado's army reached the region of Tiguex in what is now New Mexico. The Tiwa (*TEE-wuh*) tribe that lived there welcomed the Spaniards at first. But when Coronado's men needed food and blankets, they simply took them from the Tiwa. In frustration the Tiwa made the Spaniards' horses stampede. Coronado's men stormed the Tiwas' pueblo. Many Tiwas died in the battle. Others were captured and burned at the stake.

Eventually the Zunis fled their homes in fear of the Spaniards.

Coronado spent two years searching for gold, but he never found any. "Having failed to do anything more than spread destruction and disease among villagers, he returned to Mexico," according to historian Roger Nichols. Coronado left behind the Zuni, the Hopi, the Tiwa, and other tribes who would always fear and hate the Spanish.

Coronado's and de Soto's actions represented the worst of European behavior toward American Indians. Few explorers, however, ever tried to truly understand the cultures of the tribes they met. In every case, relations between Europeans and American Indians grew tense over time. Europeans tried to take the American Indians' land or change their ways of life. These early encounters between explorers and American Indians set the stage for changes that would alter the continent forever.

EXPLORATION TIMELINE

1492
Columbus makes his first voyage to the New World.

1534
Cartier makes his first journey to Canada.

1539
De Soto's unsuccessful search for gold begins in Florida.

Hernando de Soto

1540

Coronado's search for the
Seven Cities of Cibola begins
in what is now the southwestern
United States.

1608

Champlain establishes a
fort for fur trading in what
is now Quebec, Canada.

1609

Hudson encounters an
Algonquin tribe in what
is now New York City.

Glossary

alliance (uh-LY-uhnts)—a union or joining for a common purpose

conquistador (kon-KEYS-tuh-dor)—a leader in the Spanish conquest of North America and South America during the 1500s

encounter (en-KOWN-tur)—an unexpected or difficult meeting

expedition (ek-spuh-DI-shuhn)—a journey with a goal, such as exploring or searching for something

immunity (i-MYOON-uh-tee)—the ability of the body to resist a disease

inferior (in-FEAR-ee-ohr)—lower in rank or status

musket (MUHSS-kit)—a gun with a long barrel

prophecy (PROF-uh-see)—a prediction of something to come

prophet (PROF-it)—a person who tells the future

pueblo (PWEB-loh)—the Spanish word for village, usually consisting of stone and adobe buildings

ritual (RICH-oo-uhl)—a ceremony or special way of doing something

skirmish (SKUR-mish)—a small battle

vagabond (VAY-guh-bahnd)—a person who wanders from place to place

wampum belt (WAHM-puhm BELT)—a belt made from polished shells woven together

wary (WAIR-ee)—cautious, on guard against danger

Read More

Bader, Bonnie. *Who Was Christopher Columbus?* Who Was …? New York: Grosset & Dunlap, 2013.

Gunderson, Jessica. *Conquistadors: Fearsome Fighters.* Fearsome Fighters. Mankato, Minn.: Creative Education, 2013.

Krull, Kathleen. *Lives of the Explorers: Discoveries, Disasters (and What the Neighbors Thought).* Boston: HMH Books for Young Readers, 2014.

Ross, Stewart. *Into the Unknown: How Great Explorers Found Their Way By Land, Sea, and Air.* Somerville, Mass.: Candlewick Press, 2011.

Critical Thinking Using the Common Core

1. How did explorers change North America? What might North America be like now if the Europeans had never arrived? (Integration of Knowledge and Ideas)

2. If native peoples had had access to weapons such as the Europeans possessed, how might relations have been different? (Integration of Knowledge and Ideas)

3. Why did the European diseases affect the American Indians so severely? (Key Ideas and Details)

Internet Sites

FactHound offers a safe, fun way to find Internet sites related to this book. All of the sites on FactHound have been researched by our staff.

Here's all you do:
Visit *www.facthound.com*
Type in this code: 9781515718666

Index

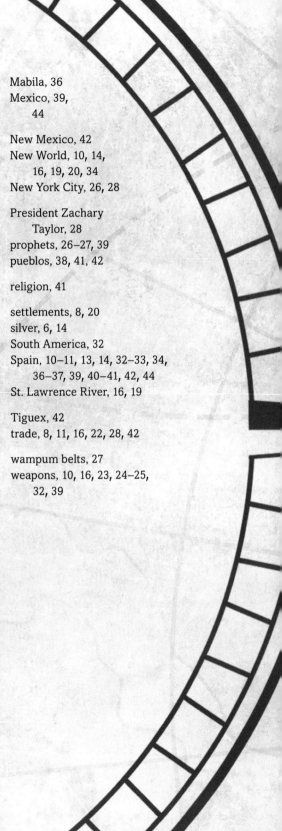